D0931673

THE UNEXPLAINED

CROP CIRCLES

BY KRAIG HELSTROM

BELLWETHER MEDIA • MINNEAPOLIS, MN

Are you ready to take it to the extreme?
Torque books thrust you into the action-packed world
of sports, vehicles, mystery, and adventure. These books
may include dirt, smoke, fire, and dangerous stunts.
WARNING: read at your own risk.

This edition first published in 2011 by Bellwether Media, Inc.

No part of this publication may be reproduced in whole or in part without written permission of the publisher. For information regarding permission, write to Bellwether Media, Inc., Attention: Permissions Department, 5357 Penn Avenue South, Minneapolis, MN 55419.

Library of Congress Cataloging-in-Publication Data

Helstrom, Kraig.
 Crop circles / by Kraig Helstrom.
    p. cm. -- (Torque: The unexplained)
 Summary: "Engaging images accompany information about crop circles. The combination of high-interest subject matter and light text is intended for students in grades 3 through 7"--Provided by publisher.
 Includes bibliographical references and index.
 ISBN 978-1-60014-583-4 (hardcover : alk. paper)
 1. Crop circles--Juvenile literature. I. Title.
 AG243.H368 2011
 001.94--dc22
                                    2010034776

Printed in the United States of America, North Mankato, MN.

010111   1176

CONTENTS

Chapter 1
A Mystery in the Fields.... 4

Chapter 2
What Are Crop Circles?...10

Chapter 3
Searching for Answers..... 16

Glossary 22

To Learn More................ 23

Index.............................. 24

CHAPTER 1
A MYSTERY IN THE FIELDS

In July of 1996, Rod Taylor steered his small airplane over the plains of England. He had one passenger with him. The ancient monument **Stonehenge** passed below them in the evening sun. Fields of grain surrounded the monument. They saw nothing unusual about any of these fields.

Stonehenge

Taylor landed the plane and dropped his passenger off. He refueled and returned to the air. Then he saw something that shocked him. One of the fields near Stonehenge had changed. A series of 151 circles had appeared in the crops. It made a spiral pattern.

Tourists began to notice the circles as well. Many drivers pulled over to see the strange shapes. Some of them said they had seen a mysterious mist in the area earlier that day.

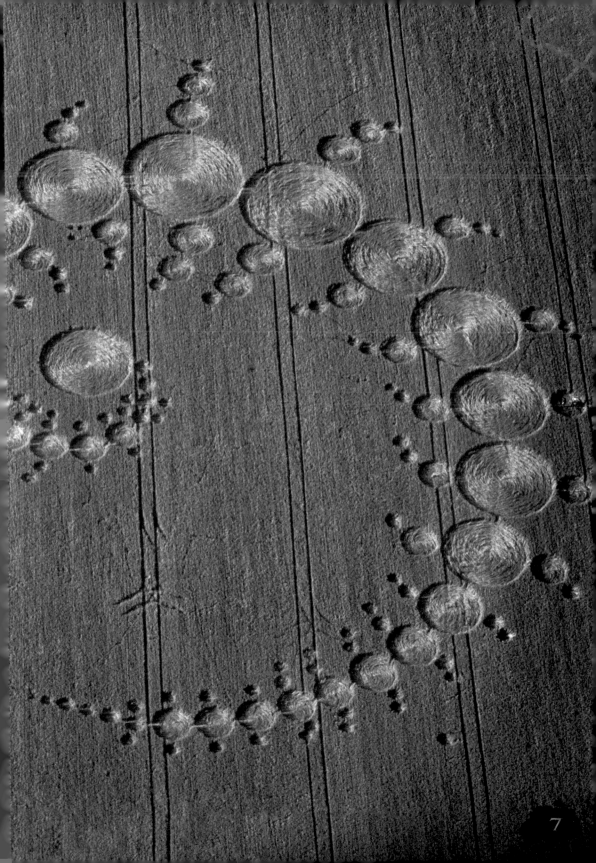

7

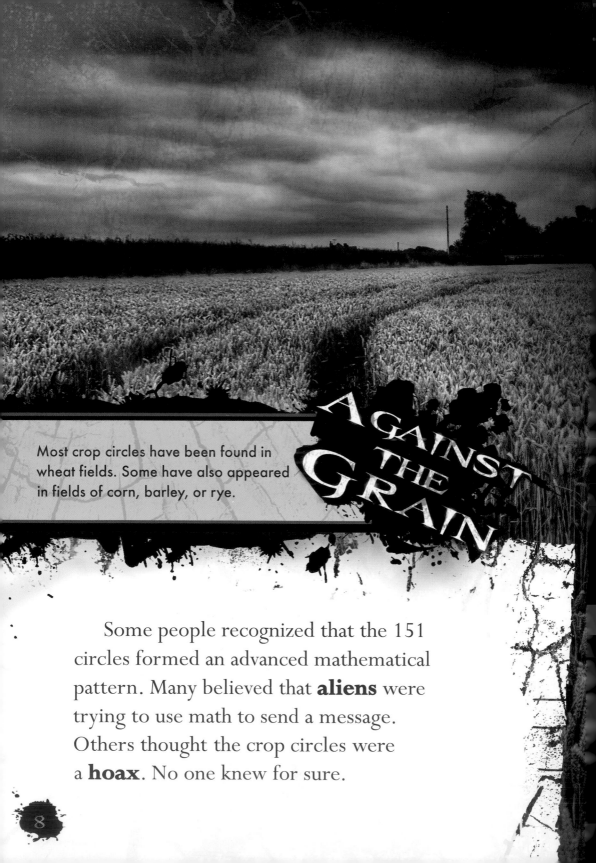

Most crop circles have been found in wheat fields. Some have also appeared in fields of corn, barley, or rye.

AGAINST THE GRAIN

Some people recognized that the 151 circles formed an advanced mathematical pattern. Many believed that **aliens** were trying to use math to send a message. Others thought the crop circles were a **hoax**. No one knew for sure.

9

CHAPTER 2
WHAT ARE CROP CIRCLES?

In many crop circles, crops are bent at a 90-degree angle. The crops are never broken, and many still continue to grow!

BEND, DON'T BREAK

Crop circles are strange patterns found in fields around the world. They are formed when crops are laid flat in a design. Some crop circles are simple circles. Others create detailed patterns. Many people believe that the circles are an alien language.

Reports of crop circles first surfaced in the 1500s. They started to increase in the 1970s. Early crop circles were simple. They became more and more complex over the years.

In 1991, Doug Bower and Dave Chorley said they created hundreds of crop circles as pranks. The British men showed how to make the circles with ropes and wooden planks. This led many people to believe that all crop circles are hoaxes. Others think some crop circles are far too complicated for people to make.

Doug Bower

Dave Chorley

FAMOUS CROP CIRCLES

Year	Place
1678	England
1880	England
1966	Australia
1991	England
1996	England
1996	England
2007	Tennessee

Description

A wood carving called *The Mowing Devil* shows a strange creature making a crop circle in a field.

Amateur scientist John Rand Capron reports strange circles in a wheat field in southern England.

Farmer George Pedley reports seeing a flying saucer while working in a sugarcane field. He later discovers an area where the sugarcane had been laid flat in a circle.

A crop circle is discovered in a field near Barbury Castle. The formation's shape, a tetrahedron, shows a new level of complexity in crop circles.

A formation of 151 spiraling circles appears in a field near Stonehenge. The formation is a pattern of advanced math.

Camper Jonathan Wheyleigh claims to have videotaped strange balls of light creating a crop circle near a tower called Oliver's Castle.

A member of a local sheriff's office discovers a 150-foot (46-meter) crop circle in a Tennessee wheat field.

CHAPTER 3

SEARCHING FOR ANSWERS

People have many **theories** about how crop circles are made. Many people think crop circles are caused by nature. Animals could be creating the circles as they feed. Some of the circles might form because of strange weather. Researchers think strong wind patterns and **ball lightning** could flatten crops.

ball lightning

Others believe that crop circles are messages from aliens. The patterns may be used to **navigate** and point to possible landing areas on Earth. The designs could also be attempts at communication. Aliens might be warning people to take better care of the planet.

ANGRY PLANET

The Gaia theory is the belief that Earth is alive and has intelligence. Some people think crop circles might be Earth's way of telling people to take better care of the planet.

Are all crop circles created by people,
or do some have another cause behind them?
If aliens create crop circles, what are they
trying to tell us? Maybe someday we'll have the
answers to these questions. Until then, we can
only watch the fields.

GLOSSARY

aliens—beings from other planets

ball lightning—a ball of glowing light that flashes briefly in the sky during a storm; ball lightning results from electrically charged gas.

hoax—an attempt to trick people into believing something

navigate—to find one's way in an unfamiliar area; some people think crop circles help aliens navigate the surface of Earth.

Stonehenge—a stone monument in southern England; most scientists believe that Stonehenge was built by an ancient civilization.

theories—ideas that try to explain why something exists or happens

TO LEARN MORE

AT THE LIBRARY

Mason, Paul. *UFOs and Crop Circles*. North Mankato, Minn.: Smart Apple Media, 2005.

Oxlade, Chris. *The Mystery of Crop Circles*. Chicago, Ill.: Heinemann Library, 2006.

Wencel, Dave. *UFOs*. Minneapolis, Minn.: Bellwether Media, 2010.

ON THE WEB

Learning more about crop circles is as easy as 1, 2, 3.

1. Go to www.factsurfer.com.

2. Enter "crop circles" into the search box.

3. Click the "Surf" button and you will see a list of related Web sites.

With factsurfer.com, finding more information is just a click away.

INDEX

1500s, 13
1970s, 13
1991, 13
1996 (July), 5
aliens, 8, 11, 19, 21
animals, 16
ball lightning, 16, 17
Bower, Doug, 13
Chorley, Dave, 13
communication, 19
crops, 6, 10, 11, 16
Earth, 19, 20
England, 5
fields, 5, 6, 8, 11, 21
Gaia theory, 20
hoax, 8, 13
math, 8
navigation, 19

patterns, 6, 8, 11, 19
Stonehenge, 5, 6
Taylor, Rod, 5, 6
theories, 16
wind, 16

The images in this book are reproduced through the courtesy of: David Parker/Science Photo Library, front cover, pp. 10, 11, 20-21; Damian Gil, pp. 4-5 (top); Jaroslaw Grudzinski, pp. 4-5 (bottom); Juan Martinez, pp. 6 (small), 9, 17; English Heritage/Photolibrary, pp. 6-7; Ant Clausen pp. 8-9; Joze Pojbic, pp. 12-13; Rex USA, p. 13 (small); Dave O'Dell/Alamy, p. 16; Jon Eppard, pp. 18-19.